LIZETTE COWLEY

YOU WERE BORN FOR THIS

The Ultimate Guide on How to Accomplish Your
True Purpose and Calling in Life, Learn How to Discover
Your Passion and Pursue Your True Calling

Descrierea CIP a Bibliotecii Naționale a României
LIZETTE COWLEY
  YOU WERE BORN FOR THIS. The Ultimate Guide on How to Accomplish Your True Purpose and Calling in Life, Learn How to Discover Your Passion and Pursue Your True Calling/ Lizette Cowley – Bucharest: Editura My Ebook, 2021
    ISBN

LIZETTE COWLEY

YOU WERE BORN FOR THIS

The Ultimate Guide on How to Accomplish Your True Purpose and Calling in Life, Learn How to Discover Your Passion and Pursue Your True Calling

My Ebook Publishing House
Bucharest, 2021

CONTENTS

INTRODUCTION ………………………………………..	7
Chapter 1. Living Your Life On Purpose ……………...	9
Chapter 2. Find A Satisfying & Fulfilling Career …….	12
Chapter 3. Understanding Your True Calling …………	15
Chapter 4. Using Your Intuition To Fulfill Your Life Purpose ……………………………………………..	18
Chapter 5. Finding Your Purpose Through Serving Others ………………………………………………..	21
Chapter 6. Are You Living Your Values? …………….	24
Chapter 7. What Are Your Innate Talents? …………...	27
Chapter 8. Your Interest And Your Passion …………...	30
Chapter 9. Searching Your Life Purpose With Numerology ………………………………………..	33
Chapter 10. Never Be Afraid To Pursue Your Purpose Of Life ……………………………………………….	36

Chapter 11. Heart and Soul Query 39

Chapter 12. Preparation ………………………….. 42

Chapter 13. Training ………………………………. 45

Chapter 14. Commit Beforehand ……………….. 48

Chapter 15. What Bravery Does For You ……….. 51

Wrapping Up ……………………………………… 54

INTRODUCTION

A lot of people today live life without having any deep connections or purpose as they are so busy looking after the daily expectations that more often than not, stopping to take stock of things is something not many indulge in. get all the info you need here.

Chapter 1

Living Your Life On Purpose

Synopsis

Chasing a career or studies or simply just immersing oneself in the daily requirements of the life cycle, does not really give anyone very much room to explore anything outside. This exploration would normally require the setting aside of some quiet time and concentration, in both body and mind and in the hectic surroundings of most individuals; this is not an indulgence that they are prepared to give attention too. Some would even go as far as saying that it would be a waste of time and effort, thus brushing aside such acts as unimportant and silly.

Discover Your Purpose

For the more discerning few, the exercise of finding one's life purpose is anything but frivolous. Finding one's purpose in life will help to give the individual a real picture of either his or her capabilities and put these into action to achieve the purpose perceived. It gives the individual the zest for life instead of just simply existing day to day on mundane and often exhausting and stressful regimens. Identifying the purpose of one's existence also allow the individual to enjoy a certain level of fulfillment and peace as the energy used to strive towards the end goal becomes well worth the effort. It also provides the individual with a concept to live by and the positive energy will help the individual through thick and thin.

People who are able to find their purpose are usually people on a mission to get the most out of their lives, and they are also usually very driven, focused and energized. Keeping healthy both mentally and physically are the common traits of those who seem to have identified their purpose in life.

Chapter 2

Find A Satisfying & Fulfilling Career

Synopsis

There are very few people who actually enjoy what they do and take pride in doing it to the best of their abilities. This is mainly due to the fact that such careers chosen are usually not done with the individual wanting to find satisfaction and fulfillment but rather to simply exist until something better comes along. The danger here is that sometimes nothing better comes along, and the individual ends up settling for just anything and eventually comes to a point where he or she is unable to get out of the rut they are in.

Find Your Path

The following are some points to consider in the quest to find a satisfying and fulfilling career while exploring all options available:

- Perhaps the first and often the most difficult step to take would be to actually seriously identify the career that might present these two elements within its package. Satisfaction and fulfillment should never be disregarded as an indulgence. It is often the most important feature that will keep the individual driven to do and be the best. Once this particular exercise is thoroughly explored, then the individual will be able to move on and look for positions that are based on this very basic finding. However caution should be exercised to ensure the individual stays realistic and in touch with the current market requirements and business trends.

- Next, there needs to be a lot of research, analysis and help exercised in order to acquire the information on the ideal position sought. This part of the exercise may include the seeking the expertise of a mentor, having dialogues with those in similar positions, having in depth discussions with career guidance counselors and other avenues of gaining information from those actually involved in the line the individual is interested in. First hand information is a lot better and more beneficial for the person who is seriously considering the particular career, for satisfaction and fulfillment elements.

Chapter 3

Understanding Your True Calling

Synopsis

Most people go through life dong a job just to get the pay check at the end of the month. Most spend nearly all of it on bills and rarely do something they actually like. Others are happy at work and have large amounts of money. However for the vast majority this is but a dream yet to be fulfilled.

Identify Your Calling

This causes the individual to lose any passion felt as the job does not in any way stimulate the mind and body to give the best possible results it can. Being stuck in the seemingly endless cycle does not encourage the individual to look to the future with anticipation and excitement. Therefore to get the best out of life itself, the individual would be required to spend some time and effort to actually explore the possibility of understanding his or her true calling and working on fulfilling this call.

The positive outcome of being able to understand the true calling has far reaching effects on the individual's life in general. Everything will seem better and clearer and the individual will eventually be able to find happiness in the most simple of things. Reaching this level of mental and physical connection is something most people are never able to enjoy through their lifetime, due to their inability to make concerted efforts to understand the true calling of their existence. Being able to deal positively and honestly with the feelings and thoughts will help the individual better identify the inner voice that is so in tune with the true calling meant for him or her. Taking the time to stop and think really hard about what really excites, stimulates and interests them will help to narrow down the quest to finding the true calling they were designed to embark upon.

Chapter 4

Using Your Intuition To Fulfill Your Life Purpose

Synopsis

Tapping in the intuitive side of an individual is not something that involves magic or guess work. Contrary to most people's thinking, intuition is actually a very real and often proven element within the human mind.

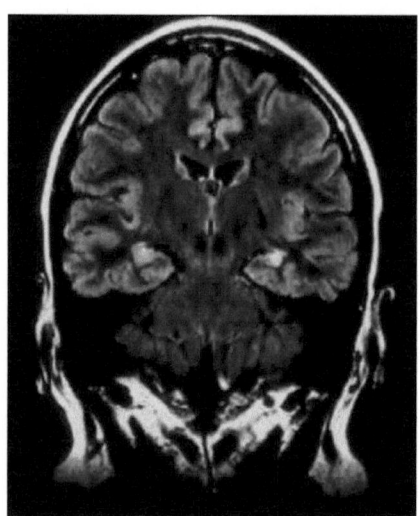

This intuition is plainly explained as the body working together with the mind to tell the individual something without the needs to use the other 5 sensors to make it understood.

Examine It Well

Intuition is usually closely connected to or associated with women, as men are perceived to be rather too "shallow" both in body and mind to be able to tap into or feel such depth the intuitions normally dictates. Feeling something without actually knowing the source of the prompting could be categorized as intuition and when an individual chooses to ignore such promptings, there are usually dire consequences to be paid. A lot of people especially women rely heavily on the particular style of seeking and getting answers or solutions to a situation or problems that is weighing heavily on their mind.

A more complex and scientifically acknowledged form would be the multisensory perception whereby the individual would claim to experience a hunch or an acute prompting about a particular element. This is a very sophisticated system that connects, with elements within and outside the human body and mind to produce enlightening perceptions in general.

With practice this exercise can be called upon and interpreted accordingly, while still acknowledging that is does require some extensive understanding which unless the individual is tuned into will not bring forth the desired results. Being able to practice being intuitive will certainly help when wanting to explore life's challenges and directions for the individual.

Chapter 5

Finding Your Purpose Through Serving Others

Synopsis

Not everyone is lucky enough to be able to indulge in the activity of finding their purpose in life, and this is mainly due to the fact that they are mostly so caught up in the daily challenges of life, that this activity seems to be always benched. When this goes on for years without any end in sight, the individual eventually loses the will to finding his or her purpose in life, and instead opts to continue drifting in life.

Help Others Help You

The following are some areas to consider, as it should give an interested individual some indication as to how one can go about finding the purpose of life:

- For some it is very easy to identify the things that make them happy and excited, while for others it may take a little time, effort and exploration. There is also the possibility that once identified, the exercise that beings forth joy and fulfillment is not measurable or accepted by society as beneficial, thus forcing the individual to rethink and perhaps even consider discarding the idea altogether. Therefore there is a fine line between indulging in frivolous activities and indulging in activities that are considered beneficial to both the individual and those around.

- Discovering the natural gifts and the joys of exploring and using these gifts to help others may eventually cause the individual to be able to identify the areas that most create passion and excitement from within. Fulfillment is usually found when the individual is able to see the fruits of labor benefiting other while at the same time enjoying the whole process.

- Exploring various different types of ways of serving people may eventually help the individual identify the one that most gives fulfillment. Getting involved in organizing or facilitating events for the less fortunate can be a very fulfilling experience.

Chapter 6

Are You Living Your Values?

Synopsis

In order to be able to effectively live by one's values, there should first be an exercise to identify these values clearly and to ensure they are the defining points of the individual's general life and the journey it takes.

You And Your Values

Most people have a few core values they live by and understand the extent they are willing to go to ensure these core values are not compromised in any way, will show the inner character of the individual. Some of these core values may include elements of honesty, hardworking styles, perseverance and many other actions or characteristics that define the individual. These values are the elements that usually carry the individual through tough situations, where decisions made are based on these values. Priorities are usually given to this mindset and judgment calls are made in line with this, thus it is important to be able to fall back on some really good and strong value systems.

The important question that should be the focus of the individual's life, would be if he or she was living life according to these values or if there were numerous compromised being made, in order to be pleasing or accommodating to others. If the individual finds that compromise seems to be the general agenda in their lives, the outcome will eventually cause the individual to perhaps become a negative person, as frustration takes hold and values are abandoned.

Therefore besides the exercise of exploring the value system the individual perceives to adhere to, it is perhaps more important to ensure these values are completely understood and practiced on a daily basis. This is what eventually defines the individual as different and help make it possible to happily acknowledge that they value their beliefs greatly. Knowing that one is living according to a value system that is part of the mind and body will definitely bring about a deep sense of satisfaction.

Chapter 7

What Are Your Innate Talents?

Synopsis

Finding one talents is something that could be quite a challenge especially if that talent is not really evident and has not surfaced significantly in any way. However exerting some effort to actually take the time to find this area of perceived gifting, will eventually help the individual to attempt to incorporate this talent into the everyday experiences, thus effectively ensuring a more enjoyable and fulfilled life.

Tapping In

There is a lot of misguided acceptance that an individual will eventually control and influence the mind and body to learn to accept circumstances and make the best of them. This may be true to a certain extent but it will not really help the individual to bring out the talents that may be hidden deep within. Most times these talents are not used simply because the individual is really unaware of its existence, thus making it impossible to capitalize on them.

Then there is also the thought process that encourages people to strive for being the very best in whatever endeavor they decide to take on. Any success is then related and connected to the perceived talent it took to bring the endeavor to its current success state. This too is not really the inner talent that is so popularity talked about.

The following are some guidelines that could be adopted in the quest to find the individual's talents:

- Being able to identify the difference between learned skills and skill that are apparent through inner motivation and drive.
- Being able to connect to something and feel really complete and comfortable without much prompting will also be another indication of the innate talent.
- Searching for jobs that would seem to suit the individual both in body and mind can only be accommodated if there is some chance of talent displayed.

Chapter 8

Your Interest And Your Passion

Synopsis

Happy people are people who have learned to be comfortable within themselves and thus have the knowledge of what interests them and what ignites their passionate side. If the individual is looking for a happy and fulfilled life, then it would be worth exploring the various ways of finding this often illusive passion and interest.

Ignite Your Passion

The following are some ways to help discover the elements that could tickle the interest and ignite the passion of the individual:

- Almost everyone is able to identify a hobby or an interest that keeps them happy, focused and feeling useful. This is a good place to start when it comes to the exercise of finding further interests and passions. Understanding that this may require the individual, to take the very important decision to step out of the comfort zone is essential.

- Being open to new experiences will also help the individual to explore other possibilities that may surprisingly ignite the interests and passion of the individual. There are many things to be learnt and experienced when making the effort to try new things and if the results are positive and enjoyable, then exploring further would be the next step.

- Communicating and staying informed of anything and everything will also help the individual come into contact with elements that could create feelings of interest and passion. There are always new developments to explore and actively participating in such exercises would be rewarding in itself.

- Facing fears is also another way to find a person's interest and passions. Often people are afraid of being rejected or turning in work that is considered below standard, thus keeping them from venturing into making an attempt at these things. Overcoming these sometimes irrational fears can unfold surprising capabilities.

Chapter 9

Searching Your Life Purpose With Numerology

Synopsis

Life in general is confusing enough, without the added confusion of having the figure out who we really are and our purpose. Most people try and define who they are, using the ever common method by linking their lives to what they do, but this does not really define the person.

Beat The Confusion

When questioned, most people respond according to what they do rather than really know who they are in terms of purpose in life. The idea is to be able to differentiate between the two and really explore the possibilities through finding one's purpose in life, and one way of doing this would be to turn to the art of numerology.

The idea of using numerology can seem to be confusing and a rather skeptical one, but by simply using facts such as the name and date of birth, an individual is able to gain some insight into the realm of finding the life's purpose. Some sources believe that numerology does help to steer an individual according to the path of life mapped out by connecting factors that may be beyond comprehension. Numerology is sometimes considered an ancient occult that helps an individual to find the direction in the life through a series of numbers and their connecting meanings which the life purpose reflects. The two types of numerology would be Chaldean and Pythagorean and these are supposed to help unlock the life directions as seemingly as a manual would.

Using the life purpose number which is basically calculated on the letters of the name, the individual would be able to learn the purpose of life based on the personality traits that might help to send the individual in a certain direction.

Chapter 10

Never Be Afraid To Pursue Your Purpose Of Life

Synopsis

Many people fail to live purposeful lives simply because they are not really in tune with their mind and body, and are nor focused in exploring the things that most ignite their passions. Getting caught up with the everyday challenges seem to force and individual to put their own personal needs and desires on hold and focus instead on just getting through life's challenges.

Live Your Purpose

However for the lucky few who are rebelling against the need to simply submit to life's challenges, there is some hope in finding and pursuing life purpose to the fullest measures possible. Understanding that the purpose in life has a higher importance when measured against achieving just goals is something to consider in the search. Ideally the purpose in life, arises from the talents and values of an individual and this is easy to decipher if these fact are obvious to the individual, however the confusion usually arises when the individual is unaware of his or her talents which is commonly confused with skill.

Still the most telling elements that can steer the individual towards a clearer picture of the purpose in life would be to connect it with valuable insights gained by immersing one's self into different activities. The comfort and enjoyment derived from certain actions will give the individual a clue as the direction toward the purpose in life. There should never be the element of fear or discouragement that should be allowed to dominate the individual's thoughts to keep the individual from trying new and seemingly impossible things. Fear is something that should not be allowed to creep into the equation, as it is often the crippling point that stops the individual from pushing limits to seek answers. Exploring and staying excited about new things will always help the individual gain more insight to the purpose in life.

Chapter 11

Heart and Soul Query

Synopsis

If you take a minute to design your day, write up your to-do list, or consider what action to choose next, stop and inquire, "Where is the course with a heart and soul?" This is potent as it will help you right away dispose of the choices that don't have a heart and soul.

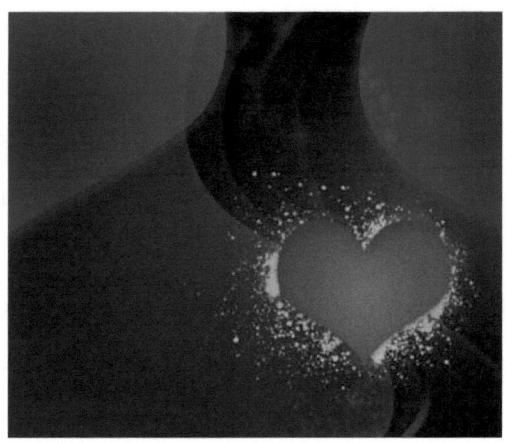

Choose Wisely

If you're sitting at home, attempting to determine how to spend your night, ask yourself the heart and soul question. Observe how particular options feel hardhearted and void, while other courses bring about a tingle of fervor when you think about them.

Let your heart and soul help you discover the correct course. Take note that the word courage is in the word encouragement. Once we identify the course with a heart and soul, we feel boosted to get moving.

Maybe rather than watching TV, you're boosted to read something that makes you fell good. Perhaps rather than playing PC games, you're boosted to have a rich conversation with your partner about the future of your love and life. And perhaps rather than simply going through the motions at your job, you're boosted to press yourself to make the most beneficial contribution you are able to. The heart centered option leads you to the course of conscious development.

I frequently ask myself this question when choosing which content to write next. Due to the ceaseless influx of reviewer propositions, as well as my own development experiments, I never have a deficit of ideas, but it may be backbreaking to pick out a subject as there are so many great ones to think about. Once I stop and inquire: Where is the course with a heart and soul? The correct topic commonly becomes clean-cut. It's the matter that frightens me a bit, the one I'm not certain I can write on well, the one that excites my soul. On those occasions when the subject doesn't get clean-cut, it's because the heart-centered course calls for doing something; different than a piece of writing.

Post the heart and soul question in a position where you'll see it day- after-day, or set it as your PC's screen saver, so you will be reminded of it a great deal.

If you ask the question, you bring your system of logic and intuition into alignment.

Chapter 12

Preparation

Synopsis

You are able to utilize the same grooming idea from that was discussed earlier in this series to step by step build your bravery. Rather than tackling your greatest concern straight off, face up to your smallest concerns first, and progressively work up to more important acts of bravery.

Get Ready

First of all, pick out a concern you'd like to overpower. It's all right if it's too large for you to take on straight off. Now see if you are able to distinguish one little step you may take to face up to that fear, something that may be a reasonably modest challenge for you but that would still spark off some type of change.

For instance, if you're afraid to start up a conversation with someone you don't know, your foremost goal may be to walk past an unknown person and grin. If that still feels too hard, begin with a simpler goal, like making eye contact with an unknown person for one minute.

Discipline yourself with your beginning baby step till you feel geared up to increase the hurdle. There's no particular number of repetitions you have to finish for every step, but 5 to 10 is a great approximate range.

Imagine you get the hang of making eye contact with unknown people, being able to control it for one full second without glancing away. You might feel a little nervous about it at the start, but after 10 repetitions, you are able to do it again and again. Then step-up the challenge to 2 or 3 moments.

When you've surmounted that, you might wish to advance to grinning.

Following, try grinning and saying hello. Inside a matter of weeks, you are able to slowly work up to beginning a conversation with a total unknown person. Every baby step builds up your experience, letting you gradually advance from beginner to expert without feeling overpowered.

Make every training step as little as you wish. Confront modest challenges that you're reasonably confident you are able to finish. Feel free to duplicate as many repetitions as you indigence to till you feel prepared for the following step. You command the tempo.

By abiding by this preparation procedure, you'll achieve deuce things. First of all, you'll quit reinforcing the dreadful avoidance patterns you demonstrated in the past. Secondly, you will condition yourself to behave more bravely in future spots. Your dread will diminish while your bravery grows.

Chapter 13

Training

Synopsis

Among the biggest fears is that of the unidentified.

Get Schooled

The fear of the unknown may be relieved by accumulating supplementary knowledge. Facing up to fears head-on give the sack be helpful, however if your anxiousness is for the most part due to ignorance or lack of experience, you might be able to cut back or eliminate it merely by schooling yourself.

Imagine you're afraid to go out of your hometown and move to a different city, even though you would love to undergo the experience. Perhaps the primary reason for your hesitancy is ignorance. The whole feeling seems overpowering as you don't know what will happen.

But you are able to learn what you have to know by studying sites, linking up with residents of other places, and taking little jaunts. The knowledge you learn will help you behave more bravely and in addition to that more intelligently.

It's awe-inspiring how many opportunities we deny ourselves due to deficiency of knowledge or experience. In this prosperous information age, "I don't know" is plainly not a valid rationalization.

All the data you require is readily accessible on the Net, in cheap books, or in others brains. If ignorance is restraining you in any field of your life, then take the first step and train yourself.

Chapter 14

Commit Beforehand

Synopsis

An easy way to build bravery is to make commitments that do not call for much bravery to swallow but that call for substantial bravery to carry out.

Decide

Once you place yourself on record, you will tend to carry out what you said you would do. Little commitments may help you overpower complacency and build up substantial bravery.

During my beginning few months as a member of a local oral presentation club, I chose to enter a funny speech competition. I had never contended in a grownup speech competition previously, however when I was asked if I wanted to take part, it didn't take much bravery for me to state, "certainly, I'll do it."

As the competition date got closer, all the same, I started to second-guess my decisiveness: What in the world have I gotten myself into here? However as I was already committed to the competition, I carried out what I said and did my finest.

Bracing myself for every round of competition was difficult work, but I had a lot of fun and likely gained ground on my oral presentation skills by the equivalent of eight to twelve months of steady club attendance. Following that beginning contest season, I felt much more surefooted and brave as a speaker, and I moved on to compete in other speech competitions.

I'm certain I wouldn't be as well-situated with oral presentation nowadays if I hadn't committed to that beginning contest several years ago. All it required to get rolling was to open my mouth and state, "I will do it."

Rather than putting off your concerns, make a commitment to confront them.

If you are afraid of oral presentation, commit to handing a speech. If you're afraid of altitudes, enroll in a rock-climbing course. If you're afraid of getting in the water, sign on for swim lessons.

Remember that whatsoever you dread, you have to sooner or later confront, including dying itself.

Chapter 15

What Bravery Does For You

Synopsis

When you establish bravery, you begin to better your personal life. Building bravery will help you take risks to a sunnier future that you commonly would not take. When you body- build bravery, you place fear behind you.

Advantages

Bravery is the procedure of accepting that you have fears, yet you're willing to discover a way to get the better of those fears and not let these concerns to take charge of you. It's all right to feel your fears at advantageous times.

For example, if a car is coming your way, swerving, you've a right to fear. There's nothing wrong with sound fear. The issue is you have to place healthy fear where it belongs and unhealthy concern out of your life.

Once you build up bravery, you'll learn to self-direct your life. You'll learn to swallow punishment and payoffs graciously. A brave individual will frequently feel motivated to assume blame and responsibility while critiquing their actions and utilizing what they learn to move ahead.

Brave individuals will step to the front, instead of withdrawing when chances come their way. On the other hand, a brave individual will step back and consider his or her errors.

Occasionally the brave individual is spontaneous. It's never good to plan every day, as no one knows what the following day will introduce.

Consider it. How many times have you designed something all to see it fall apart? For example, you plan to go to a ballgame tomorrow.

Tomorrow a snowstorm, hurricane, tornado, wind storm, or rainstorm may change that. As you can see, designing isn't always in your favor, which is why brave hoi polloi are occasionally spontaneous.

An individual willing to better their life will relax. This individual will loosen up even when plans go bad. For example, if it rained on ballgame day the individual will find something else to do and feel even as happy about that.

To become successful and better your life you'll have to learn how to trust your instincts. When you do, you can trust other people too.

Alas, we live in a world where trust is difficult to find, yet when you trust your intuition, you can't blame other people when things fail.

Wrapping Up

Don't sell yourself short by not living your life by its purpose. It may not be easy to identify what exactly your life's purpose is, but once you have discovered the purpose, it will be well worth it. Those who have found their lives purpose live much happier lives than those who choose to just get by day by day. You deserve to be happy! Start living life with purpose now!

Bravery is a choice. To be brave is to face up to your fearfulness with the might that comes from your deepest associations.

As you direct your life into alignment with reality, affection, and might, fear's grasp on you will gradually soften.

Reality helps you see through the fancy of fearfulness, so you are able to maintain command over your life. Affection prompts you to intensify your connections and accomplish the unafraid state of unity.

And might supplies the power to act despite fear, building up bravery in the process. Regardless how hard it might appear, decide to confront your fears consciously.

Do not pass away without embracing the venturesome course your life is intended to be.

You might go bankrupt. You might go through failure and rejection repeatedly. You might suffer multiple bad relationships.

However these are all mileposts on the course of a life lived bravely.

These are your individual triumphs, carving a deeper space inside you to be filled up with an abundance of pleasure, happiness, and fulfillment.

Be afraid if you have to be; then muster up the bravery to follow your aspirations anyway. That's power undefeatable.

Printed by Libri Plureos GmbH in Hamburg,
Germany